MY FIRST SPORTS

Golf

by Ray McClellan

BLASTOFF! READERS 4

BELLWETHER MEDIA • MINNEAPOLIS, MN

Note to Librarians, Teachers, and Parents:

Blastoff! Readers are carefully developed by literacy experts and combine standards-based content with developmentally appropriate text.

Level 1 provides the most support through repetition of high-frequency words, light text, predictable sentence patterns, and strong visual support.

Level 2 offers early readers a bit more challenge through varied simple sentences, increased text load, and less repetition of high-frequency words.

Level 3 advances early-fluent readers toward fluency through increased text and concept load, less reliance on visuals, longer sentences, and more literary language.

Level 4 builds reading stamina by providing more text per page, increased use of punctuation, greater variation in sentence patterns, and increasingly challenging vocabulary.

Level 5 encourages children to move from "learning to read" to "reading to learn" by providing even more text, varied writing styles, and less familiar topics.

Whichever book is right for your reader, Blastoff! Readers are the perfect books to build confidence and encourage a love of reading that will last a lifetime!

This edition first published in 2011 by Bellwether Media, Inc.

Library of Congress Cataloging-in-Publication Data
McClellan, Ray.
Golf / By Ray McClellan.
p. cm. – (Blastoff! readers: My first sports)
Includes bibliographical references and index.
Summary: "Simple text and full-color photography introduce beginning readers to the sport of golf. Developed by literacy experts for students in grades two through five"–Provided by publisher.
ISBN 978-1-60014-461-5 (hardcover : alk. paper)
1. Golf–Juvenile literature. I. Title.
GV968.M33 2010
796.352–dc22 2010000791

Printed in the United States of America, North Mankato, MN.
080110 1162

Contents

What Is Golf? 4
The Basic Rules of Golf 8
Golf Equipment 14
Golf Today 18
Glossary 22
To Learn More 23
Index 24

What Is Golf?

Golf is one of the most popular sports in the world. Millions of people love trying to hit a small golf ball into a cup.
It is thought that modern golf started in Scotland a few hundred years ago.
One belief is that it came from a game Scottish shepherds played.
The shepherds knocked stones into rabbit holes.

Golf has grown a lot since it was invented. People began making equipment just for golf. Thousands of courses were built.

fun fact

The first modern golf course was St. Andrews in Scotland. The course is still in use today.

By the early 1900s, golfers traveled around the world to play in tournaments. Soon millions of people around the world were interested in golf.

The Basic Rules of Golf

A game of golf is played on a series of holes. Each hole starts at the **tee box** and ends at the cup. A golf course has 9 or 18 holes. Every hit of the golf ball is called a **stroke**. The goal is to get the golf ball from the tee box to the cup in as few strokes as possible.

Scores are measured by **par**. This is the suggested number of strokes a hole or course should take to complete. A golfer who takes 3 strokes on a par 3 hole has "shot par." A golfer who finishes in 2 strokes has shot "under par." A score of 4 or more is "over par."

Golf Scoring Terms

Hole in One: Finishing a hole with just 1 stroke

Eagle: Finishing a hole 2 strokes under par

Birdie: Finishing a hole 1 stroke under par

Par: Finishing a hole with the suggested number of strokes

Bogey: Finishing a hole 1 stroke over par

Golfers begin each hole by hitting the ball from the tee box. They try to hit it onto the **fairway** or the **green**. They try to avoid **hazards** such as sand and water. On the green, golfers try to **putt** the ball into the cup.

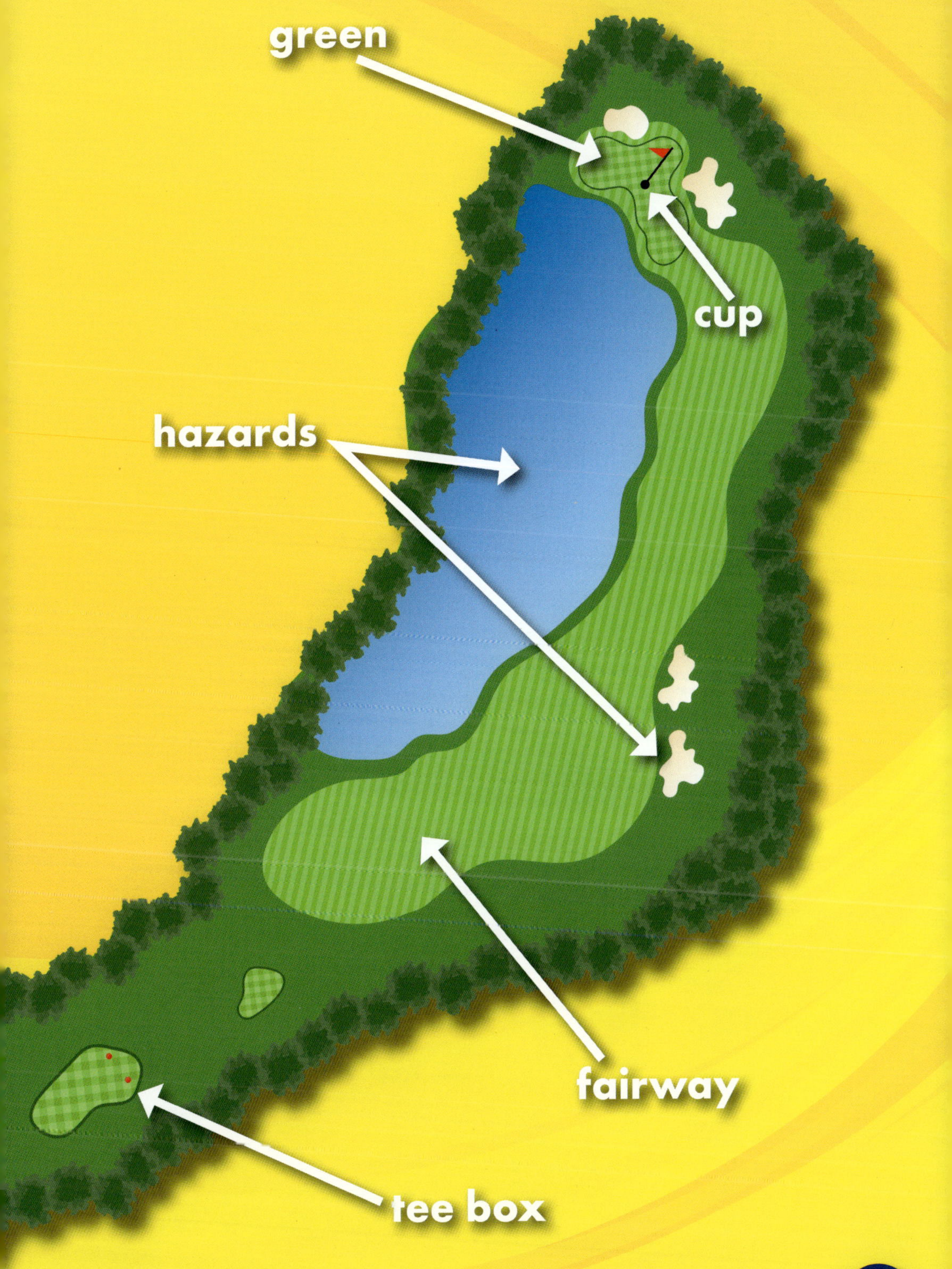
green
cup
hazards
fairway
tee box

Golf Equipment

Golfers need golf balls and clubs. A golf ball has a solid rubber core. Some golf balls have rubber thread wound around the core. A cover with **dimples** surrounds the core and thread. The dimples help the ball fly farther.

fun fact

A new kind of golf club is a hybrid. It is a combination of a wood and an iron.

Golfers carry three main kinds of clubs. A **wood** has a long **shaft** and bulky head. It is designed to hit the ball low and far.

An **iron** has a shorter shaft and a small, angled head. It is for shorter, higher shots. A **putter** is used on the green to roll the ball into the cup.

Golf Today

Golf is popular with men and women of all ages. Most people play for fun. Some take the game very seriously. Golfers hoping to become **professionals** must attend **qualifying school (q-school)**. The top 25 finishers at q-school can play on the Professional Golfers' Association (PGA) Tour. Women play on the Ladies Professional Golf Association (LPGA) Tour.

The biggest PGA tournaments are called **majors**. Golfers play a course four times. The golfer with the lowest total score wins.

fun fact

Winning all four majors in one year is called a grand slam. No modern golfer has ever done it.

Golfers who win majors often started playing golf when they were young. Do you think you could one day win a major?

Glossary

dimples–small indentations on a golf ball; dimples help a golf ball fly farther through the air.

fairway–the short grass that runs from the tee box to the green

green–the very short grass that surrounds the cup

hazards–obstacles such as sand traps or water that get in a golfer's way as he or she tries to reach the green

iron–a golf club with a short handle and a narrow, angled end; irons are used for high, short shots.

majors–the biggest tournaments in golf; the PGA Tour has four major tournaments: the Masters, the U.S. Open, the British Open, and the PGA Championship.

par–the suggested number of strokes a golfer should take to complete a hole

professionals–people who are paid to play a sport

putt–to hit the ball on the ground, over the green, toward the cup

putter–a club used to putt the ball on the green

qualifying school (q-school)–a school for golfers who want to join the PGA Tour; golfers need to finish in the top 25 at q-school to get on the PGA Tour.

shaft–the long, narrow part of a golf club that connects the grip to the head

stroke–any strike of the golf ball

tee box–the area at the beginning of each hole where a golfer makes the first stroke

wood–a golf club with a long handle and bulky end; woods are used for long, low shots.

To Learn More

AT THE LIBRARY

Kelley, K.C. *Golf.* Ann Arbor, Mich.: Cherry Lake Publishing, 2009.

Smith, Ryan A. *Golf Balls: From Start to Finish.* San Diego, Calif.: Blackbirch Press, 2006.

Thomas, Ron, and Joe Herran. *Getting into Golf.* New York, N.Y.: Chelsea House Publishers, 2005.

ON THE WEB

Learning more about golf is as easy as 1, 2, 3.

1. Go to www.factsurfer.com.
2. Enter "golf" into the search box.
3. Click the "Surf" button and you will see a list of related Web sites.

With factsurfer.com, finding more information is just a click away.

Index

1900s, 7
birdie, 11
bogey, 11
cup, 5, 9, 12, 13, 17
dimples, 15
eagle, 11
fairway, 12, 13
golf course, 6, 7, 9, 10, 20
grand slam, 21
green, 12, 13, 17
hazards, 12, 13
hole in one, 11
holes, 9, 10, 11, 12
hybrid, 16
iron, 16, 17
Ladies Professional Golf Association (LPGA) Tour, 19
majors, 20, 21
par, 10
Professional Golfers' Association (PGA) Tour, 19, 20
professionals, 19
putter, 17
putting, 12
qualifying school (q-school), 19
scores, 10, 11, 20
Scotland, 5, 7
shaft, 16, 17
St. Andrews, 7
stroke, 9, 10, 11
tee box, 9, 12, 13
tournaments, 7, 20
wood, 16

The images in this book are reproduced through the courtesy of: Bob Grieser, front cover, pp. 9 (small), 12 (small); Chad Ehlers/Alamy, pp. 4-5; TopFoto/The Image Works, p. 5 (small); Richard Ross/Getty Images, pp. 6-7; Matt Apps, pp. 8-9, 11, 14-15; Peter Titmuss/Alamy, p. 10; Donald Sawvel, pp. 12-13; Andrew Barker, p. 15 (small); Juan Martinez, p. 16; Sri Maiava Rusden/Getty Images, p. 17; Richard Heathcote/Getty Images, pp. 18-19; Kevin C. Cox/Getty Images, p. 20; David Cannon/Getty Images, p. 21.